READY WRITER
BRITTNEY CHARISSE

To every artist who has doubted themselves. Every writer who's talent has been minimized. Every poet who hides behinds the pen. Every spoken word artist who feels alive at the mic.

To Aunt Tweekie, who believed in this project since I was 14. Thank you for making me believe that this was an attainable goal.

To Charity & Anthony: May you pass this down and may it keep going to add to the legacy of creativity that's inside of you-no matter how that may be executed.

Contents

Foreword

What do people expect from their poets? I believe one expectation is to write what is careful, nothing without conviction or truth. The second would be to write what is useful, if pain is a doorway then let reflection be key. The third, write what is meaningful, nothing without passion or purpose, nothing that lacks consequence. The fourth would be to write what is provocative, nothing that commands no response. The fifth would be to write what is beautiful, rather that be wonderful or wistful, sometimes the perfect day on the beach or merely the silver lining in the cloud.

I think all of these things also tease out what people expect from their ministers, their friends, their family, their spouse, their mothers, and the truth is it is a process to be any of those things in any given moment. The beauty, not only in this book, but as I've watched the part of the journey I've been present to is I've seen you be any and all of those in any given moment. In 2016 Collective Verite was just an idea I shared with Dieufaite after work, no members, no name for it, but a vision that felt prophetic and soon coming.

In 2017 as we finished our first show through much frustration, tears, smiles, and joy I saw what felt prophetic become tangible. The endless open mics, the late nights of all of us bonding, our table talks where we allowed vulnerability. I watched you explore life and yourself in those moments. In truth, most if not all, prophecy is understood in hindsight and so although I had no notion of name or members you are exactly what the Collective needs for its function. We often talk about our poetry and words being ministry to others but the Collective most fruitful ministry might have always been to each other. Since we have formed we have been there for each other on our best days and often our worst, and that's what it means to be a village

To read your journey through this book and remember the days and the conversations that birthed these moments seems more like a design than a recollection. You've negotiated so much to become both the artist and human I know you to be. It speaks to a level of perseverance, trust and submission to a higher calling.

In your life many things have changed, many people have left, and it brings back to mind a line from a poem.... One day all this pain will be useful to you. You may be living in the day, or string of days, where all the pain and all the joy have become useful to you and you've made poetry of it.

Or something like that, but what do I know, I be wilding sometimes. Also thanks for introducing me to my wife.

-Dejuan Bland
Collective Verite

Preface

I began writing at a very young age through journaling. I would document my day as I got older, as if I was placing history on the pages. At some point journaling turned into a love for poetry. Story telling flourished into an artist expressing the emotions behind the stories. It was as if a light switch flipped and I was able to piece together these metaphors and themed sequences.

As much as I want to minimize what you are currently reading as *just* a poetry book, it is not. At fourteen I finished my first book, one person believed in me and sent me the materials for self publishing and said "let's get it done, you can be a published author now." I remember carrying around a legal size orange-yellow envelope with my book, asking friends to read it; getting the courage to show my father my finished material; and submitting poetry to competitions. Some how that drive to publish poetry got lost and although I continued to write my focus went elsewhere. As I entered college those journals became a reference point for growth, the envelope no where to be found. Most of the poems forgotten, but new pieces would develop over the next several years.

As a spoken word artist you know that the audience will only hear what you say in the moment, but what's written is forever. I wanted to give people the opportunity to journey through my words and take in what's being said instead of it being a short experience.

The mystery behind the metaphors can be seen in tangible writing and I'm excited to be able to provide that for some of the pieces I've performed and others that have never been spoken over a microphone.

On the same day, in 2022 two different friends in two different places called me within five minutes of one another and said the same thing: "Have you ever thought about publishing your poetry?"

Well, here it is,

What you are about to read is far more that just poetry, it is my life journey, the pain and love, the why, the drive behind the pen.

I

Introduction

Before the Microphone

I wanted to start off this book with a piece that I've never audibly shared. My father passed away in 2009. Only a year prior did I recite my first poetry piece as spoken word. When writing this piece I dramatically said that this would be the last piece that I would write. Thank God there was no life given to those words. While I didn't perform again until 2013, I did attempt to write several pieces but would only end up with single stanzas. This was obviously not the last piece I would write, but it was the end of a style that I don't regret leaving behind me. I jumped at the opportunity to write this poem for my father's obituary as a means to honor him and all that he had done for me in my life. What I want readers to note is how this was a comma where I was trying to put a period. As you continue reading please take in the growth of me as an artist in content and execution. If there's anything that you are attempting to bury, pick it up and keep going, you never know what type of growth you'll see. This was beginning to a vulnerability in my writing that I didn't realize it at the time.

Daddy's Girl

Dad always said "I'm not going to be here forever, and when I leave from this earth you're going to have to hold it together."

So he taught me the ropes of life and gave the best that he had, stepped up to the plate I know others would have.

A strong example of what a REAL man should be, set my standards high at an early age so I wouldn't bring home just anything. Everyday of my life he was hard on me, but it's what I needed to be the woman I'm called to be.

He was always there to support me in everything that I did, and to keep a smile on my face, giving me drive to live, to my fullest potential, and accepting nothing less; everyday reminding me that I was truly blessed.

Seems like all he knew how to do was to give and give.

He spoiled me rotten, but taught me how to obtain it and gave me the wisdom and knowledge of how to sustain it.

He said don't cry over my grave with an "I should've or

could've."

So I'll cherish the moments we had every day of my life
not going through life focusing on pain and strife.

But I'll always focused on keeping my head on straight.
Knowing one day we'll meet again at heavens gates.

II

Reconciliation

Before the Microphone

I had grown to despise poetry because it required too much thought. Free writing as I call it was more appealing for the past few years, it flowed more easily. As I worked on my memoir I noticed that story telling became a natural ability for me. So I began taking the the "safe" route instead of being pressured to intentionally creating word play, thematic stanzas, and content that would give the "wow" factor. Poetry only feels good to me when it isn't forced. When there's no expectation and when my pen is free to take random concepts and build. In my frustration of not wanting to be confined and forcing myself to commit to poetry, I found my love for it again. Here you will see the conflict between artist and art. To be artist, is to be crucified, scrutinized, and bare. To be artist is to be exposed, no protection. We are no saviors, we are living sacrifice.

Don't Call It a Comeback

Sometimes this pen be like a long lost relative that lives on these pages from my distant hometown. Familiar but disconnected.

I found myself saying "If I never write again, I think I'd be ok." Because I've fallen in love with writing my heart without the constraint of metaphor.

Lately, I've been seeing art as prison with no reform for the pressure to perform.

The dread of producing fire without spark had engulfed my home of creativity.

What I had once found as a refuge for my musing is now fresh foundation inviting me to build again.

Because as you can see…I can't help it.

But, don't call it a comeback.

Call it revival, reconciliation, reunification.

Or you can call it covenant because these words sometimes threaten me with divorce.

Seems like we always fight our way back to one another.

Remembering the smiles at similes and worry over word play.

We remember the stages.
How good what we put together sounds in rooms of welcoming ears.

How the amplification of that microphone loves to intertwine itself with acoustics that make stories come alive.

We remember the release of weight, and how communicating this art be our bridge over our bump in our union.

We remember when we first fell in love, our why. Our reason.

Our love, our memories, and we stay a little longer until our next fight.

Ready Writer

They say what's written is forever, you can't take it back. The
pen is eternal, infinite, permanent.

It's movements classical.
Sometimes flowing lightly, sometimes minor, but never small.

It's bold, brave enough to etch the unthinkable, strong enough
to tight rope on lines in the sky.

Flexible enough to be trapeze, or cannon ball,
It can create circus.

The pen is sharp making the cleanest cuts with the smoothest
lines.
Illuminating what's hidden.

But it's sometimes in the darkness that the pen is ready.

It brings light. It Digs.
It uncovers broken treasure to be pieced together by speech.
To be extracted by the tenderness of tears.

To delicately research the fossils of the past.
To be archaeological, to be anthropology, to be historian.

To time travel, and put story to artifact and explanation to age
old art.

Sometimes the pen is ready to be scientist, and meteorologist
to predict the next storm.
To forecast what the human eye can't see from coast to coast.
It tells of a shore that has been violently washed with harsh
waters.

This pen tells what's to come and where it's going.
Sharing stories
It pushes the wisdom in the weary for those traveling the same
road.

The pen, though permanent, is timeless. Always ready to add
to archive.

Before the Microphone

My most skillful word play piece. This is one piece of a 5 part poem with Collective Verite. We received an offer from one of our members for a group piece. I did not want to be out-written, knowing that word play hasn't always been my strongest skill in writing I was pushed to do my best and this is what came of it.

I Write

I write in pencil to go viral, penicillin.
Penciling in the led to takes breath away.
Sketching vivid illustrations in black and white.
Using colorful colloquialisms to hit the culture just right.

Just writing in red ink, heart bleeding through the
papermating with metaphor.
When I write, its my date with destiny so just *R.S.V.P.* for *G 2*
to the wedding.
They ask me how vivid my dream *B.I.C.* a future with me and
word. It's etched permanently with *Sharpie*. We gel pent up
emotions into overflowing fount pens.

We flow effortlessly like calligraphy.
We go back like Old English, polishing and finishing splinters
into beautiful Mahogany.
We carve catch phrases and hit them in the mitts of the crowd.
People asking for recipes and secret ingredients, I tell them we
don't have to use seasonings because the word flows perfectly
just like Bland.

When I'm dull Word sharpens me, we're committed until

death because even after eternity the Word is still left.

III

Beginnings

The pieces in this section are the beginning of my spoken word journey. I've always been a writer, but it wasn't until college that I learned what spoken word was. In this section you will be able to see my progression as an artist and the shifts between my styles of writing. This transformation as an artist was freeing. I began to focus less on the audience response and more on the skill of writing. I'll never despise my beginnings; however, I'm in love with where and how I've grown.

Before the Microphone

In workshops or panels on writing, I'll often say that I have drawers full of random pieces of paper that have one stanza or one line. Sometimes phrases or word play will come to me and I'll write it down so I don't lose it. The cool think about storing away those thoughts is that I can come back and piece together a poem later. The first stanza in this poem was written after my father passed away. I finished it years later and this is what came of it. As a musician I seen life as a song with many dynamics, a classical piece with many twists, turns, and moods. Most of all this piece is evidence that your pain can be turned into something artistic.

My Song

Pain had my gift imprisoned and I'd grieve at the mention of
pouring out again to be used as an instrument

With hammer weighted keys. As every scale and arpeggio
weighed down on me staring in crisis the key of c, death d,
bitterness b, and the sustaining pedal must have been held
down on g, grief.

I couldn't understand how I was expected to echo the sounds
of praise, when I had been tuned to create pitches of loud
frequencies that reflected my pain.

Tuned to complain.
Tuned to give off vibes that gave feedback of my screeching
cries.

Tuned to produce loud beats that blew me away from serenity
I could not longer reach the heights of musical tranquility.

And as I climbed the scales I fell flat with every sharp chord
that wrapped itself around my neck.

Perhaps I had been trapped in some composers sad song.

Who was this author?
He was the finisher of my song faith and his word began to
intertwine with the sound that I was making, I was mistaken a
beautiful song was being created.

No! This was not the work of satan.
Never could he come up with something so divinely
orchestrated complex nor creative.
This was my life, time signatured by God and the more I was
pressed I was impressed that each measure held something
immeasurably more than I could ask or think.

Peace in the midst of my sorrow and the jagged stabbing pain
of staccato.,
My sad ballad was being turned into worship, legato.
Every major key event began to make a minor sound.
It was no longer forte loud.

Just as I thought it was ending,
the ds al coda took me back to the beginning.
What first looked like a complicated song filled with 16th and
32nd notes was now beginning to flow.

Every break of every beat, every measure that held repeat, was
now working out for my good and his glory.

It produced his song and my story.

Who is this author?

Jesus.
He's the finisher of my song faith.
This can be referenced in Romans 8:28

Before the Microphone

Looking back on this next piece I honestly can't believe I won first place in a poetry competition with it. Although "My Song"was written first, this was the first piece I performed after coming back to spoken word in 2013. I don't have much of a back story on how or why I wrote it, but I remember going to an open mic night on campus at the University I attended. I sat in the audience and was too afraid to try to put my name on the list. Well, a friend of mine who I hadn't seen in maybe four or five years was there and talked to the host. My. name was called and I won the first place in the competition that night. I'll always appreciate that push. It was at that moment that I knew I had something special and I stopped being afraid to put myself out there. It's difficult to share these early pieces because they aren't my favorite style of writing, but it is my hope that throughout this section you can see the obvious progression of my writing.

Rebellion to Redemption

I was driving the roads of my life trying to write my own story. God saw my fatigue and instead of being a passenger who handed me food or drink when I was in need, he saw the destruction I was headed towards and still insisted on taking the wheel.

Two people can't drive at the same time and I was too busy indulging in my joy ride, driving the wrong way on the wrong side, pride.

He was yelling and screaming my name, but I had turned up the music refusing to sing his praises, insisting on driving in circles and mazes instead of the long narrow road that God gave me.

I found that I had made a deal with the devil. Instead of boldly pursuing God's will for me I wanted to still do pieces of my own just to see how much I could hold on to. There were a few things I couldn't afford to lose. I refused to give up me for Christ, So i held on to my will with all of my might.

Always keeping in mind what I could do to barely stay saved, you'd be amazed how quickly the enemy put me in a daze. The passions and desires for my will set ablaze.

The flames spread quickly and swiftly, instead of being on fire for God I was now on fire for me.

I had so many things that I wanted to go right, looking at things through my eyes instead of Christ's sight that saw the destruction I was headed towards; backwards into the enemies arms instead of forward.

But God, who's so rich in grace and mercy refused to let me mess up his name.
He began to remind me that like Israel I bore his name, that I was proof that he existed.
No matter how many twists or turns I took trying to get to the promised land there's no way he would allow me to miss it.

As bad as I wanted to fit in with the idol worshipers in their midst, I would always look like a misfit.
He snatched me out of Egypt and I felt like a reject, but it was okay because I was being rejected by the world.

It regurgitated me because it's system wasn't accustomed to something that was different. I began to sing a new song of repentance for my resistance.

Before the Microphone

I'll be honest, while writing this book my older poems didn't cross my mind. During editing this poem came to mind for my "beginnings." One of the first (and last times I performed this piece I butchered it. I'll never claim to be a perfect artist, it's just tha tover the years I've learned how to strategically continue through a stumble of words. I honestly don't remember the thought process behind this piece, I think I had become someone I wasn't use to after being taken advantage of too many times in a short period. My stance on forgiveness is seen here as I process through the effects of harboring negativity. Unforgiveness and bitterness is a serious disease. If you don't let things go it can affect your health and mind. It can cripple you from moving forward, and cause you to forfeit connections or community out of fear of past hurts happening again. It's always been easy for me to forgive and move on, but at this time issues were piling up and this provided an outlet to untangle a web of emotions that had sat for months and get back to what I believed.

Heart Issues

My heart had been infected with offenses and my mind
couldn't really make sense of why it created fences that
prevented forgiveness and repentance.

I tried to use man made cures of sweeping things under rugs
and pretending it didn't happen, but the infection had spread
and I needed a heart transplant.

My bruised battered heart could no longer withstand pain and
be covered with a bandage.
I was sensitive to any touch that could potentially be a hazard.
My actions even showing that it had been damaged.

It wouldn't pump Christ's blood that I had been infused with
so that that I could love unconditionally.

Instead it began to condition itself to it's deadly conditions.
Offenses began to mount and infectious cells rose in count.
Pulling me in a cell where irritation, anger, and rage prevailed.

Cardiac arrested by the enemy so I couldn't grab, grasp, I was
gasping for air that needed to flow freely to my mind so that I

could not rehearse, wrongs done to me, my thought process
needed to be reversed.

Then I was shocked by the paddles of Holy Spirit that said,
everything that happened to me could be equated to how God
had been treated by me.

And instead of secretly or openly holding on to it, he cast it in
the depths of the sea.
If I was truly made in the likeness of Jesus then that means I
have the capacity to love like him unconditionally.

It was recommended that I exercise to maintain my healthy
heart. Lifting weights off of me to my father, and when it gets
too heavy he's always my spotter.

Now Psalm 51 is my prayer: "create in me a clean heart, and
renew in me the right spirit." Don't take your love and
presence away it's what guides me and leads me by grace.
Please never again let offenses close my mouth, but allow it to
shew forth your praises.
I'll go on loving like you, declaring that your grace is amazing.

Before the Microphone

I love the versatility of certain pieces, this next piece is one of my favorites to add as an introduction to "I Will Meet You" or "Why Don't they Love Us." I originally wrote this for an event in my hometown after having a dream about the city. A message for Christians to focus on what God is focused on instead of man made doctrine and made up rules; this poem is a call to prayer to fix the root of problems instead of surface level conflicts that really have no bearing on a real action plan of change. Throughout this book you will see different styles of writing that may be difficult to understand on paper. That is because some were written as performance pieces. For Example, the third line in this piece says "I whispered it the first time because that's how loudly some of us are portraying Christ." This line is present because during the performance I use the repetition to get the audience's attention.

Dim Lights

Jesus is the Lord and Savior of my Life.
I said Jesus is the Lord and Savior of my Life.
I whispered it the first time because that's how loudly some of
us are portraying Christ.
Controlling Christianity with a dimmer, and we don't shine to
bright because we say things like:
Her dress is too short, his pants are too tight, you can't sit in
that row, your praise isn't quite right, your lipstick is too
bright, and you might distract the pastor from seeing Christ.
We have indeed, become creatures of an environment that
wasn't supposed to have man made boundaries.
Many of us pleading to be free from a structure that keeps us
bound by law in religious captivity.
Christ is saying "please church take the limits off of me."
Where the spirit of the Lord is there is supposed to be liberty.

This is what was portrayed to me in a dream: I was riding
down the street and what i saw were nations with blood
crying out loudly.
Heart wrenching deafening screams, grieving fathers, sisters,
and mothers drowning out the voice that says "Where is your
brother?"

Cain are you Abel to take responsibility for your actions? Yes
you are your brothers keeper that is not past tense, and the
church is sitting here saying "how do we get past this?"
The truth of the matter is we cannot blame, shame, or hate if
we have not properly shown them the way.
So this is what God has to say: "if my people who are called by
my name would humble themselves , pray and seek my face;
then will I hear from heaven and heal their land" and they will
stand with hands that are no longer blood stained and
proclaim victory in my name.

Before the Microphone

I was sitting on my bathroom floor in college because that was my quiet space at the time. I wanted something new. I wanted a fresh encounter with the Lord. This was a time in my life where I was in robotic routine, and while routine establishes discipline it also made me feel as though what I was doing on a day-to-day basis was not authentic. I cried out to the Lord asking for a new type of encounter with him and at that moment my prayer began to change, and this poem was birthed. Ironically…or not, this piece would be what was used for my first out of state poetry performance. I began to realize how much of a gift poetry was, when I previously thought it was just something I was good at. I left Michigan as "just a poet" and returned as a spoken word artist.

One Night With the King

I couldn't miss this.
I seen him coming and caught a glimpse.
It was Jesus, from Nazareth.

So I, like blind Bartimaeus
Cried "have mercy on me oh son of David"

A beggar in spirit, begging for attention and prescription for
my sickness.
And yes, they stared.

Even though they were blind to my blindness the one thing
they could see was that I was unclean
So the audacity of me to try to approach his majesty.

But if I would've allowed church folks,
I mean Pharisees
To stop me
My life would've been a tragedy.
So I pressed, struggled, and screamed
Savior, Son of David have mercy on me.

He turned around to say "what is it that you need?"
My King I just want to be free.

And at that moment I could feel religion being stripped from me
I could see the veil being ripped for me
And I was able to enter his presence as a priest of the king.
Finally able to see what the Psalmist could mean when he said;
'better is one day in his courts than a thousand elsewhere
because the feeling I felt there couldn't compare to the best
feeling on my best day.

So when he said go on your way you've been healed by your faith I couldn't help but to stay.
What manner of man is this that causes the winds and seas of my life to instantly obey?
My faith, began to operate and move to another beat.

Since I could see, my "help my unbelief" turned into "thank you Lord,"
My "thank you Lord" turned into "help me to help others see."
My "help me to help others see" turned into a place where I could intercede and my intercession for *them* turned into intercession for me.

I began to rehearse who he was to me. God Almighty,
Everlasting, Jehovah Nissi,
Jehovah Rapha, Jehovah Rohi,
Wonderful counselor, Prince of Peace,
Name above all names,
And the one who delivered me.

He said "it is because of me not things that you decided to seek,
no good thing will I withhold from you because you strive to
walk righteously."

What are you expecting from the king?
He said "seek me and I will add all things.
Anything is possible to them that believe."

Before the Microphone

"I Will Meet You" was the beginning of me getting out of my "rhyming" phase. I started to focus on the skill of using metaphors instead of making sure that everything rhymed. As you will see in this piece, I did pick up the rhyming in the scheme with the names of God. It was the "safe" choice in bringing this piece to a close. Writing this let me know that I had the skill of creating themes and metaphors to hold the theme together. The foundation of this writing is based on God meeting me where my fear and lack of faith had overtaken me. This is a picture of the growing belief that God is with us even in the scariest moments. I was believing God for a promise that was taking years and in the moment he reassured me through this that he was right there all along. I remember being excited writing this, it was as if God and I were writing together. I started to see poetry as ministry, and it was a beautiful marriage between passion and God-given gift.

I Will Meet You

I couldn't see.
The vision you gave me to focus on had become blurry
And the fog was making it hard to see what was in front of me.

That is when I heard you say "you aren't supposed to be
walking by sight anyway and that is why we need to meet."

I will meet you where the lack of your faith in the
impossibility will turn the possible into definitely.

I will meet you where the fear that has terrorized you meets
my perfect love that forcefully casts it out.

I will meet you where the uncertainty of situations turns into
certainly you are called to be what I've called you to be before
Let there be Light, before Genesis and before Darkness. I will
Meet you

I will meet you where the earthquake of your life meet my
rushing wind causing a tsunami of my glory.

I will meet you in our secret place where I often find you

crying out to me on your face displaced from the storm.

I will meet you You the heaviness of you meets the rest of me.

Where there's a transaction and the weights of your life can be cashed into me.

I will meet you where the pieces of your broken heart meets the peace that surpasses all understanding

Where sorrow is turned into joy that you can continuously enjoy.

I will meet you where the worry that tries to consume you is consumed by the testimony of the sparrow who I watch over.

I will meet you where your stumbles collide into the rod of the word and align your steps into destiny.

I will meet you where your "I am weak" is swallowed by I AM. Where your "I am in need" is consumed by I AM

I will meet you where the issues of life roll of your tongue and crash into my mighty voice

I AM that I AM

I am Rapha I am Rohi

I am God almighty

Everlasting and Jehovah Nissi

I am Shalom, I am Jireh

I am the Lord of Hosts, I am the consuming fire.

I am Jesus, I am the way, I am YAHweh

I am that I am, and I will meet you.

I will meet you where this moment meets the victory I won with you in mind.

I will meet you

Before the Microphone

When I first heard the song *Reckless Love*, it felt like my first time really believing that God loved me for real for real. I began to look at my life and remember all the times I attempted to self-sabotage, all the times that I caused my own storms, and how God really came through for me. I remembered the casualties of sacrifice. Those relationships that didn't work out. the closed doors, the idols, and the ties to my will that kept me from getting closer to him. A review of someone not letting anything stand in the way of their love and perfect plans for you is sobering. It made me think of life as a city that I built, that had to be destroyed and rebuilt so that he would be my first love.

Reckless Love

I once rode a beautiful wave that coasted me to an island of
self.
Once tasted privilege so satisfying that it fulfilled my appetite
for what I perceived as eternity.
Once touched a mirage of success
Once realized I was holding my breath
Once found comfort in chaotic dysfunction
Once sought refuge in the perishable.
I once drowned in my own tears, on an island of self.

I leaned on concrete to stabilize the shakes of life.

Built skyscrapers that were empty inside
acres that held no value.
Made mountains out of life, invited nomadic as settled
structure.
I built a city on an island with a foundation of sand.
Soiled in confusion.

One day he destroyed everything to get to me.
He waged war for my soul.
Casualties and unbearable grief

Digging valleys and hiding in the darkness of trenches.
Running from shadows into the darkest corners

And now I stand.
I stand In a city wrecked by battle.
The sky seems gray with smoke, and the dust is settling.
Most days it can be unsettling. I see the world through dark
colored frames, every building's architecture seems
abandoned through my vision,

But now I've fully grasped the revelation of the church as his
bride
Understood the relentless pursuit that a groom would produce
for the apple of his eye
and I've learned to find beauty in His destruction.

Minute Musing- How Great is Our God

How Comforting is your embrace that blankets concerns and initiates rest on the pillows of your peace

How encouraging are the words of he who wrote this story before the thoughts of conception.

How wide is the ocean that swallows the microscopic issues of the land and washes away the rocks & stone that were thrown before grace.

How persistent is the love of the one who stretched out, reaching for humanity, releasing blood as sacrifice.

How patient are the hands that lift the heaviest chains.

How strategic are the plans of he who mapped out the creation of the universe.

IV

The Struggle

There are times in my life where I feel that people only see what I can do for them and not me as a person. Writing through those moments help me to release what I can't articulate in normal conversations. As an artist people see the gift and marvel at it and often don't listen to the words you are saying. Or, it's easy for others to try to use the gifted instead of seeking the source. The frustration of being a servant, but still needing to be served creates an internal friction.

Before the Microphone

There was a time in my life where the demand on my gift was running me into the ground. It's important to be self-sacrificial with your gifts, but sometimes it gets frustrating. I have come to know this: You have to serve because you have a heart of service, not because you're expecting the same thing from the other person. When I wrote this I was serving with a thought in the back of my mind that said, "because I do things for others, I should be receiving repayment any day now." However, the word says that we should work as unto the Lord, that sometimes means that your reciprocity will come from him and not from people. We have to settle in that. People aren't required to repay what was given to you (gift) for free. The gifted must reconcile that we will be rewarded in heaven for some things.

Invisible

She bares herself before people only to be told to put on
clothes.
Vulnerable and disrobed
And they only want to see porcelain white molars painted
pretty on a canvas that She puts up to decorate.

But they ask if Shes ok.

Now I know what you'll say...
She should be more careful about who she exposes herself to.
But maybe people shouldn't ask; in a world absent of
transparency.
Absent of structures with strength to hold weight.

Unprepared for no.
just wanting a show.

So She dance and sing and paint pretty pictures.
She dances and sing and paint pretty pictures.
I dance and sing and paint pretty pictures.
I dance and sing and paint pretty pictures.

Until broken records be too much to bear.

And even with a savior she wonders if she'll be ok.

If one day…
Correction won't turn into tortured condemnation

If one day…
the "you're not alone's" will turn into manifested presence

If one day…
She'll be able to feel without crying

So…to make stage of herself…she
Says:
Don't be afraid to look in the mirror.
It could be a bearable sight today.
Deep breath.
Put on face.
Exhale.

Before the Microphone

This is a complicated chaotic piece of writing, and it's intentionally written to read that way. As I grew older I noticed that there was a lot of unlearning I had to do when it came to my relationship with God. A lot of what I learned was religion and the traditions of man, but there was no real knowledge of who God was and his character. While being consistent in church culture I had also become robotic, and disingenuous. This piece paints a picture of a church building that is somewhat of a circus on the inside but has noticeable attractive features that can draw a curious mind in. You will also notices some undertones of truthful voices being muted at the realization that they are playing a game of religion without a real relationship and the detriments of doing so.

Robotics

You know what it feels like to run for your life?

It's like: Deep Breaths. Look both ways. Seek shelter.

My hands touched creaking door, feet touched dust from a
strangers past, and my eyes captured beautiful ruin.

Brick and mortar with stained glass windows, that made me
unable to see the outside,
it hypnotized. I seen people who were hypnotized

Chain gangs with rhythmic movements to
The drum of overseers footsteps.
They begged me to dance with them, and we became slaves to
beat.

Repeat, repeat, repeat, repeat.
Dawn to dusk
Morning to Night
Sunrise to sunset
Light to dark

Same movement danced with different sways
Same words said with different phrase.

Same place.

I forgot….that I was seeking refuge
And found myself hanging…from a noose…from a tree with
no fruit…as soon…as they tried to press mute…on my Truth…

But a tree with no fruit, is one with dead roots.

I mean a building with no foundation is one that can crumble

I mean religion,
I mean ritual without spirit
I mean repetitive-non scriptural motions

Is a recipe for natural catastrophe.

I found that:

We take residence in housings prone to diminish in stormy
winds
And we trust in what's easily shaken in earthquake.
We hope in what gets twisted in tornadoes
And what gets washed away in hurricanes.
What gets overcome by tsunami
And burnt by volcano

We've made temporary comfort. And trusted in what's easily
weathered by the storm.

We've deposited our hearts in something that can't withstand disaster

Straw and stick houses were easily blown away so we found security in brick and mortar.
The big bad wolf couldn't destroy it.
We've adopted a pigs theology.

Just because the house isn't easily broken with strong wind, doesn't mean that hasn't collapsed on the inside..

Minute Musing- Finessing Stress

I always thought I was late to the game,
Maybe that's why life got delayed.
Felt like I Shot shots with no assists, it was only in *my w*rists.

So when I got injured I still wanted to play.
But they made show out of my pain.
Slam dunked word play, triple double on the similes, and made
3 points to bring my subjects to a close.

Guarded my problems, thought God was center but I couldn't
move forward
Seemed like I was always giving my all with a full court press
Seeing how well I could hide my weakness so others could be
blessed.
I was finessing stress.

But that's all they taught her
She couldn't play organized, more like a Harlem globe trotter.

Now I'm one fifth of a five man team
I'm in the locker room with all the greats and we got about five
rings.

V

Land Wounds

Traveling

They Say Don't Grow Weary.

But tell me, tell me how does a people who have been running in different directions for centuries not get tired.

We've ran north only to build ceilings to rooms we're reluctantly invited to.

We've ran in the south tilling the ground that holds roots of racism in this land.

We've ran west for them to appropriate the rich culture in our blood.

And we've ran east to try to make a home in art.

As much as we've ran you would think we would have a gold medal by now.

You would think that we would have surpassed whole continents in boxing, in track, in gymnastics.

You would think the fights, the cross country running, and hoops that we've danced through would make us champions of this nation.

But in all honesty, it seems we've been disqualified from these Olympics.

Maybe they know we'll just keep coming back strong.

Maybe they've found that in their drive to muzzle, to mute, to suffocate that we'll still find our voice.
Because I've seen us bend with flexibility that should have broken us.

I've seen us forgive with hearts of gold that should've been arrested unto death.

I've seen us try to pry blind eyes wide open with the jaws of our own lives.

But I believe that we Weill keep running,
Keep fighting.
That we'll keep jumping through those fiery hoops with resilience.

I believe in our resilience.
I believe in our brilliance

And even though these bodies.
These vessels of God-given strength scream with exhaustion.

Our minds…
Our minds will rejuvenate easily AGAIN for the journey
ahead.

And maybe we won't run.
Maybe we'll walk into this next victory.

Before the Microphone

I have a love & hate relationship with the next piece. In 2016 I was in prayer with some friends and I was reminded of an officer that had been involved in a murder of a black man at the time. While in prayer the Lord led me to pray for him. I had no problem praying for him but what I noticed was, what I stood for was in direct confrontation with the Lord's instructions to pray for our enemies. This poem is the conflict of culture vs. belief. The conversation of being black, knowing that injustice is still very prevalent but still recognizing that it will never be fully eradicated without the help of God. Those are my beliefs anyway. Of course we can be angry at injustice, we can protest, we can march but we also cannot allow it to make our hearts bitter. I still struggle in performing this piece because I'm imperfect and this conversation with God was a very hard truth to sit with.

Why Don't They Love Us

I recently consumed the hardest pill I've ever had to swallow
and it didn't go down smoothly. It was more like the bitterness
you taste from un-coated aspirin. Not as sweet as the sugar
coated pill that makes disease taste just as sweet.

No, this medication corrected wrong education, I was sleeping
and it awakened me. I thought I was so conscious, but I had
fallen fatigue to what it really means to be a Christian.

This prescription aborted my mission, realigned my loyalties. I
heard him say "you're royalty. Not just because of your
ancestor's bloodline, but because of Jesus' blood that
transcends time." Many of us think that we are woke but we're
really blind to what justice really means, Jesus is on our side.

My reply was "Lord Why? Why don't they love us?"

Don't get it twisted, I don't speak from ignorance. My
criminal Justice degree taught me that the root of policing
organizations in urban destinations was to keep a certain
population under oppression. So, no this is not a new
obsession because it seems that no matter how hard we speak

properly, wear battered hearts on our sleeves, or flash our
degrees, it does not make us exempt from the repetition of
history.

It does not give us hope for the dawning of a new day, and
Jesus interrupted me to say "Love Anyway."

I said "but Sandra, they…"
Love Anyway
"but Milton, did you see the way….?"
Love Anyway
"but Tamir, he was just a kid."

He said that doesn't take away from what I did, the stripes that
are on my skin compare to the bitterness you feel within.
When someone hurts your brother or sister you have to let me
in, you have to let me win.

But "when will we win?" He said I was wounded for your
transgressions, violations of laws.
Bruised for your iniquities those injustices I saw, chastised for
the peace that I sought to bring.
Yet you still find it hard to believe that I am He who delivered
an entire nation by parting the Red Sea.
I am He who heard Abel's blood crying from the ground.
You have to believe that I hear the sound.
I hear the sound of your communities and I'm saying unite
with me.
My love is key.
My love that has drawn is everlasting.
My love executes justice that is not just for us but just enough

for everyone.
My love wins every battle tuning into every channel watching
things that your mind cannot even fathom to perceive.
My love conquered the heart of Saul who had purposed in his
heart to kill you all.

My love conquered even the stoniest of heart in you, and if
that is not enough to prove;
Please refer to the greatest injustice of all time.
Mine.
Signed,
Jesus Christ.

VI

Love & Stuff

Before the Microphone

One Night is the most courageous poems I've ever performed. I looked in the mirror one day after a six-year long situationship and saw how beautiful I was. I took time to love my smile. I admired my skin color, my eyes, my personality. Everything that person had grown to be seemingly annoyed with I looked in the mirror that day and LOVED it. The truth was whether they liked it or not, I had to live with me. I had lost myself, completely diminishing my truth. I lived a lie settling for the complete opposite of what I knew I wanted because I valued the companionship over my actual desire. This was a moment of redemption for me, freedom, and true self-love.

One Night

One night,

I stood on the biggest stage I had ever graced.
And when I didn't see your face

What should've been the best night of my life…turned into the
biggest fit of rage
I had ever seen myself through.

At that moment I realized that I had given too much of myself
to you.

I longed for you to love me.

In my mind one day
There would be this great revelation of my love for you not
bound by conditions.
And my love wouldn't be blind, it would be the greatest sight
that you had seen.

Your eyes would be open to how I fought for you
and my battle wounds

would award me your Purple Heart.

But you didn't know that I had crowned you king. You didn't know that I had clothed you with coverings and bore your cup to protect you from poisonous intentions and whispers

You didn't know that your words sent orders and broke hearts canceled dreams and created poverty in my heart

And I thought I believed that reconciliation was not as foreign as the distant lands of Antarctica but your heart grew cold and left me in shock (this may be a reach)

All I wanted was to love you

But you said I lived in a world of butterflies and sunshine like my joy agitated your turmoil.

Like my dreams violently awakened you from nightmares.

Like my peace disrupted your lightening and thunder, your raging storms.

Like you liked the dark and I was afraid of if.

And my smile, that so many have pegged as the greatest detail on *this* canvas....you shot daggers and left it crooked on my wall of shame.

But one day…

This twisted piece of sculpture caught a reflection of flawed imperfection and saw the beauty in herself.

Realized the textures of her heart could only be mirrored by he who saw value in art.

One day…

This mahogany finished framed…was polished

And the picture was replaced.
With a capture captioned…you're worth it.

You're worth long conversations, affection, and consistent pursuit

You are the snatching of someone's breath and CPR reviving them with love.

You are the brightness in their eyes when they see you.

You are more than text messages, worth face to face communication.

Worth long hours of diving into dreams, aspirations.

Worth being called beautiful

Worth the "I was just thinking about you"

Worth being heard.

Because your picture queen, is worth more than 1000 words.

Your very careful internal and external display is worth verbs.

Before the Microphone

I was always hesitant to write love poems while single. There's a vulnerability in writing about something that you fear may never happen. From my point of view, to love is a faith move and faith and fear cannot co-exist. One will always be more prominent than the other. To have a section full of love poems, most of which were written before I was married; is my decision to free fall into love.

Teddy Baer

I used to dream of writing love poems.
For split seconds I would want to write fairy tales about this
Prince Charming.
How this sleeping beauty was finally awakened to love, and
how his wit would open my mind to the unimaginable.

I saw memes that said: "get you an artist, on your worst day
they'll find poetry in the knots of your hair"

And I found poetry...I found it in a bear.

I was given a gift.
It was a life-sized teddy bear,
With a basket of fruit.

It bore fruit
Each had a name that described its nature:

Love
Joy
Peace
Patience

Kindness
Goodness
Faithfulness
Gentleness
Self control

I was sold.

Some thought it was obnoxious, others feared it was too good
to be true, and some couldn't even see the fruit.

I saw it as a reason to write poetry

My eyes would take inventory of his face,
the royal structure of its frame.
It's reference to Africa's past
He is the unimaginable.
His eyes are diamonds.
Found in the clay-soil color of his skin
In them is all of the clarity.
They shine like the reflection of the sun.
They're open like windows in Victorian houses

He's structured on unmovable foundation.

His arms are like bricks…they make a home of safety and
warmth around my fears.
But even with that,
I'll never forget the feeling of confusion.
It was so free, I tried to make monster out of it
Until I heard God say:

This is what healthy feels like.
There is no sickness from the thoughts of the unknown.
No fences.
No boundaries.
No tensions
No *fear* of what the future holds.
Only hope.

This gift.
A bear.
Full of life.
Comfort.
With eyes that bring clarity,
To make the make-believe…believable.

Before the Microphone

"King" is one part of a four-part poem "Black Love" by Collective Verite. We wrote this in a way where it can be performed separately and together. Throughout this piece I highlight common misconceptions and lenses that others see black men through in comparison to how his community may see him. Seeking to validate and affirm; my intention is to show that in safe spaces he can flourish, exhale, and be honored instead of constantly on guard.

King

When I see you,
I see royalty.
I see sun kissed skin and rough hands that have toiled and
treaded through the building and breaking of rocky roads.

I see a boy. A boy that was never allowed to be a boy...forced
to be a man but still called boy. Forced to understand, the
complexity of adult things because there may come a day
where his face would lie on the pavement that his ancestors
paved before him.

When I look at you,
I see a strong back, that was never meant to carry the weight
of the world on its shoulders, but you carry fear and pain like
boulders.

I see the smile behind the frustration. The brightness of the
face that you've masked is what illuminates my love for you.
You see it as weakness but it is your greatest asset. It is the
proven fact that your endurance cannot be broken

I love to hear the softness in your tone when you speak to me.

Even the strength and power in your vocals chords tie me to your heart and calms my insecurities silencing me. Be vulnerable with me.

I'll let you lead, I'll dance to the drum of your beat and let you sing your own melody without switching keys. No matter what they say submission is not foreign to me. So don't be afraid to speak or disagree.

The mere presence of your masculinity is only intimidating to those who fear they will crumble next to you. I will willingly crumble next to you, you can let your guard down too.

The truth is...I'll never understand what it's like to be you. To be used. So I pray for you harder than I pray for myself...asking that God would not let your eternity greet you with a bullet or that your "intimidating" stature would not turn you into a monument or statue.

They love carbon copies but hate the real you. You are more than enough. The first edition is always best.

You are the best. Quality. Beautiful, tenacious and persistent. Don't let them tell you any different.

Before the Microphone

Earlier in this section I spoke about the fear of writing love poems. It's funny how I didn't start to perform love pieces until I met my husband. This is the comparison between my husband's logical brain and my creative brain. I don't bring logic to the table. Although I don't often think logically, I found it crazy to fall in love the way that we did, and he found it normal. It takes faith to fall in love and not get up. True love surpasses all fairy tales and what you thought you wanted or needed.

Use Your Brain

You told me that you found me in the lyrics of love songs.

I knew I found you as lost dreams in the crevices of love in my heart.

Pushing through cardio.
I hate exercising but I was Searching for truth,
exhausted and seeking sincerity... there I was...I guess, I was running.

But like a trainer, you strategically taught me to pace myself, I was actually afraid to lose...but you changed my loss by starvation into healthy gains.

And you made hopeless collide with hopeless romantic

Crazy in love met asylum, heart jacketed straight for one another

Restrained to tears because my heart was saying I love you but my mouth didn't want to birth it prematurely

Too good to be true and fairy tale are presently solidified promises from the past, and they sets lies on fire combusting them into particles parting ways from the mind bound by fear

If perfect love casts out all fear then true love must push you off the ledge to fall in faith

Now we stand in what we hoped for praying that it can be seen.

Where the sparkle in our eyes sparks flames of fire unconstrained by conditions.

You removed the statute of limitations on Love
Two law abiding citizens turned rebel surrendered to our parent, never having to prove their case for a jury of men, because the evidence made it evident.

Now we fly free only at the mercy of our faults, but grace helps us to favor our favorite things about one another above our mistakes

I tell you to use your words, you tell me to use my brain
I tell you that words come from the brain
You tell me you're no poet
I tell you I don't want you to be
You tell me it's a feeling
I tell you to use your brain to use your words

You expressed my flaws as perfection

And you, you pieced together a poem that even I couldn't write.

Before the Microphone

This is the poem that played before I walked down the aisle at our wedding. I guess you could say that it's a culmination and full circle moment to *Teddy Baer* and *Use Your Brain.* When recording it, I teared up. I believe that was the only time I've had happy tears when reciting a piece. I wrote it in a way to express what my prayers were for our marriage and lineage. Throughout you can read declarations and prayers for our children to see what healthy love looks like. I'm so grateful to have lived to not just write about what I dreamed love would look like, but to live it.

Forever

I want to write love poems about you for the rest of our lives.

I want to prove that love isn't just word play with you.

And it's so undefinable it's too big to just be a haiku.

I want to Assimilate similes comparing our love to forever.

Turn metaphor into a monument remembered down
generations of our bloodlines time

In other words. I want to bring what some think is fairy tale to
life.

For those after us will marvel at our endearment
To our great great grandchildren we will tell the story like a
fairy tale.
Our great grandchildren will look up to us as heroes for love
in a world of brokenness.
Our grandchildren will sit at our feet and ask how we met
And to our children we will be the proof that true love does
still exist.

They will brag to their friends about how their parents have
been married for fifty years.

They will tell stories of how you always speak to me in the
sweetest of tones
How I always supported your dreams
How they heard you pray for me
How they heard me pray for you
How they heard us argue but only saw us fight for our love.

They will remember us playing the staring game, our eyes
locked on our future

How we heard one another's thoughts before articulation

And touched each other's hearts with more than mere words.

How God gave us a sense of the of the future and how we
tasted the sweetest victories

Our children will define us as the sweetest of loves.

But I,

I will tell of how this poem was written before our eyes met
one another.

How it was only a spark that I hoped to one day finish.

And How you completed each sentence.

Each stanza with your love

I will tell how it was only a small seed hidden in my heart.

how I prayed that it would grow into someone with branches
big enough to cover me.

And strides long enough to follow, until the end of our days

I will tell how your footprint is something I gaze upon.
You made imprints all over my life but never left me empty.

I will tell of how God gave me someone to look up to when the
world knocks me down.

And together we will tell the world to love again.

Minute Musing- Better than Dreams

This is more than mere fairy tale or dream come true.
This is infinity, eternity, interrupted skyline intertwined.
This is God's answer to prayer storming earth.
This is love draped in wealth in a love impoverished world.

VII

Roots

Before the Microphone

This is hands down my BEST performance piece. While it is one of the darker pieces that I've written, I was able to master the proper inflections and emotion behind each stanza and transition. I was shooting a video for "Ode to Stevie" at the cemetery and I looked at all the weeping willows around and that is how the thought process for this began. I've lost a lot of family members and I started pointing out where all of them were buried and as an unhealthy coping mechanism I began to laugh and say "wow, I guess it's kind of like a family reunion." I had also just been introduced to Alysia Harris' poetry, I thought that her writing was so beautiful and raw. It motivated me to challenge myself and expand the strength of my writing without the safety structures that I had in place.

Family Reunion

Flesh once lived where bones find their home now. Eviction into coffins that confine what was once known as tangible love.

Family reunions held in dark places with weeping willows for the weeping and soft ground for the sleeping.

Tears blend into waterfalls, pools that hold a lifetime worth of human rainfalls

Our memories are silent here.

There are no hustles, just slow paced regression back to dust.

No electric slides, just manual movement through progression of grief.

In fact the only dance that we do is "ring around the Rosie…ashes to Ashes, dust to dust they've all fallen down.

The smell of barbecue does not grace my senses any longer… we pass on that and then re pass at the repast after they've passed because death has taken our hunger.

The sound of generations laughing is now silent. They slumber.

Mother never sees mini-me running and playing, does not see personality similarities or the mirrored heart and smile

Grandma doesn't rest in lawn chairs with her face adorned with smile, father does not playfully test her as though he was still a child.

I can't see that big grin on her face. As her grandchildren argue over who's her favorite. That cheese of pride, when asked who made the sides.
I can't see it.
Who…Who's to say it hasn't turn Skeleton.
That was dark.

It's dark here.

No rattling of bones…just silence.

But that willows branches…they sing.

They sing groanings and melodies
They sway heavy weighted droopy with grief but

It's deeply rooted and alive. Or maybe it cries.

Maybe when those tears fill your eyes…and your breath is

snatched away by pain…maybe your tears water its roots by the grave.

Maybe…maybe the weeping willow tries to weep for you…tries to cover you when you're left exposed.

Playing songs of hopeless lyrics that ask can these dry bones live. The answer is definite, but the question is when Will eternity meet broken hearts

Before the Microphone

I spend most of my writing speaking of the positive parts of my father. However, this is the realization of our parents' trauma and pain. Growing up my father was a functioning alcoholic. I was conflicted in knowing that his stressors when not drinking made him irritable. On the other hand, when he was drinking it made him more palatable. Here I marry the ideas of life with my father as a storm that we dance through together. Sometimes scary, other times fun, but all of the time loving. Here is where I want to highlight the importance of forgiveness for parents or guardians who didn't always get it right. I didn't realize how much my father had gone through while raising me until my aunt pointed it out. He was newly married, lost his wife, had to raise a daughter on his own, lost his mother, a brother, aunts, uncles, etc. My father also had a very stressful job. For a moment, if you're struggling with how you were raised take a second to take an inventory of some of the hardships your parents might have gone through while having the pressure of getting parenting "right."

Drunk Dad

My friend came to pick me up one day and said "wow your dad is really drunk."

I hung my head in shame and if black could turn red my face would've been bloodshot like his eyes

To my surprise she said "don't worry my father used to do the same two step."

And I said...
My father likes to dance in the rain,
Through dark clouds he'd meringue

He'd electric slide through troubled waters
And hustle with bad girls through tornadoes as if he didn't have his own twister.

His steps would wobble through hurricanes
His speech would slow roll carefully through a tsunami of inflections.

He was having the time of his life through different seasons of storms.

And I would stand in the ruin of the natural disaster.

I would pick up debri,
That's not something a child should carry

Sometimes we would drive through the storms when he
needed more music for his dance.

When he needed the beat to drown things out, we'd navigate
the troubled waters.

We were storm chasers

There were flash flood warnings

Sometimes we would get caught by the eye of the storm. But
they'd just place crown on his head and tell him don't forget
"you're royalty"

Because he had a badge of honor, authority.

I would wake him most mornings, because sirens would fall on
deaf ears.
Never alarmed..As he slept through elevated waters, he was
submerged in grief.

He, like some would get well rested by the sound of thunder

But I'm terrified of thunder to this day

Well, I guess it depends on what day.

Because I've seen days where nightmares took precedence over sunshine

Where there would be withdrawal of my joy.

When the storm was over, day would not be peaceful. I wouldn't see a rainbow.

I'd see rage.
I'd see dust storms from dry spells.

So the temptation would put song in My heart.

"Day after day I stay locked up in my room."
Because who knew what would come at day break.

So I prayed.

"I know to you, it might sound strange but I wish it would rain."

And I would pray for the rain again.

I would ask God that he dance again.

Because addiction made him more flexible.

I thank God his dance didn't kill him as a result of my prayers, because they were answered.

But He doesn't dance anymore.
And I pray he found rest after his Dance-a-thon.
Like I pray he felt relief like I felt after the song ended.
Knowing that the storm was over.

Before the Microphone

If you haven't noticed by now grief shows up a lot in my writing. I wrote this piece on Father's Day of 2017. I decided to focus on the things that I loved about people that I'd lost rather than the thought of losing them. This was pivotal in the way I processed moments of grief. There was a blog I wrote titled "rehearsal." I noticed that if I rehearsed sadness on certain days, that's what I would experience. I made the switch to rehearsing good memories and it changed my life. In regard to the poem, my father and I loved Stevie Wonder, his nickname was also Stevie. I was able to take the lyrics to song and combine them into poetry I also wrote this to where I can sing parts of the poem as well.

Ode to Stevie

Stevie left me wondering how a man could have so much strength and heart in the same shell. How a man could look past and love past flaws.

So I take a pause;

Thinking back to when I, was a little...

Long haired, chocolate girl.
Lost in the lack of my words and mountains of my thoughts, he serenaded me with unconditional love.

And *I wish those days would come back once more.*

For so long of those nights I prayed that you would never leave my side.
I knew I was the *sunshine of your life and forever you'll stay in my heart* although we are an eternity apart.

I heard stories of how you sang *isn't she lovely, isn't she wonderful, isn't she precious, less than one minute old.*

And from one minute to 21 years old, I didn't have to *worry about a thing.*

Even days before you took your last breath, you made reference of how you stood by my side as I struggled to catch mine and now we had switched places, I was on the other side,

And all that was left was the music. Like India Arie looks up to Stevie. I remembered and looked up to you.

I remembered and your words rang true, it replayed to me that I was n*ot the average girl from the videos, and my worth was not determined by the price of my clothes.*

You played that song until it played out, until I believed it. That all i needed was my guitar...but you said keyboard, pen, and paper.
You made life's song relevant to me.

And when I spoke of my dreams.
You said baby girl...do anything. Do anything between the law and bible to reach them so you reach them.

You made me find God on my own.
It was never forced down my throat.

But in you I seen
what a real relationship with Christ means.

As you held on to your chain and said it was the reason you needed to make it home to me everyday.

Our picture engraved you swore you weren't brave but you
said that it was only by Gods grace that you made it out

That is when I learned the difference between relationship and
religion
others didn't understand your pain and why you drank but
you understood that your strength was only in him, even if
you didn't always verbalize it.

So Stevie,

Thank you for the music.

Your music is the reason I am the woman I am today,

Thank you for your music.

Minute Musing -Porches

I remember we had the best views
I remember that music used to boom.

The windows rattled glass like snakes in grass.
I would get lost in beat while they would get annoyed.

Those two chairs told stories like movies on fast forward. I
just wanted the time to fly like those insects in the shrubs
nearby to their destination.

The porch seemed like prison then.

It was a vacation spot all the uncles and aunties would
frequent and they were my ticket to the store, to around the
corner, to the park. They freed me.

Now I know it was planting ground, my roots grew there.

VIII

Fun Stuff

Before the Microphone

As said in Part 1 (Reconciliation), after having children I found it difficult to make writing a priority and fall in love with it again. I had no desire to be on stages or be consistent in my craft but I knew that I had to. I asked Dejuan (the man who wrote the foreword) to hold me accountable to writing one poem per month. A part of that accountability was writing prompts sent to our poetry group and both of the next two poems are results of me challenging myself to get back to it, think outside the box and create on a level that had become unfamiliar. Kylo Ren was a challenge on being empathetic to a villian, and Brave was a challenge to write about what being bran meant to us. My most uncomfortable moments as a poet are when I'm given tasks or topics. I prefer to write about what I'm passionate about spontaneously. Discomfort often breeds growth and that's exactly what happened with these next two pieces. A bonus point is that they were written in under 24 hours which is not my norm.

Kylo Ren

Kylo Ren.
I mean Ben.

I get it. It's hard to be bright when darkness is in your blood.

Let's be honest, most of us have this family thing messed up.

You know the memes that lay claim to your mama's side being so great. But there's always something hidden in the line.

See I was trained by the light too, although surrounded by darkness. So it was never easy for me to fit in. Actually let me be honest, some people only taught me what not to do.

But I learned that everything isn't so black and white, not so clean cut.

When there's two opposing sides fighting for you

darkness can never consume light, it can only make it dim. It can only stifle its illumination, can never snuff it out: Light can always be ignited , but darkness will always be stagnant.

I know what it's like to be at war with the dark side always
trying to find the flicker of the candle in acres of midnight.
Trying to find that spark. Wondering if there's any good left to
salvage.

Thank God for those Reys of sunshine that come right at the
start of day.
Thank God for the eyes of those who care.
The heart of those who see.
The will of those too determined to let their glimpse of good
in our character go.

Don't feel guilty They say my mothers ambition to meet me
could've been what killed her too.

But even the Bible says there's no greater love than to lay
down your life for a friend

I've found that love will always be that pull back to foundation.
Thank God for those people who seemingly haunt us with
their expectation of our own capabilities.

May God bless you for your sacrifice that coerced my own.

May the force be with you

Brave

Now I know they said that brave was that little girl Merida
with the gorgeous red hair…

But can I submit my definition?
Like most it's complex.

On the days I feel brave I also feel fear.
I feel adrenaline.

It's like plummeting off of a cliff into the beautiful waters
below.

Those waves carrying you to an unknown destination

to navigate dark forests and admire the greenery at the same
time.

To walk stealthily through your nemesis' territory.

To run through quick sand.

To stand up in trenches. To catch arrows. To dodge bullets.

To be brave is to know your shelter may sometimes not be visible.

To hear the leaves ruffling and continuing to let this game run its course

To be brave is to have faith. To trust without sight.
To pretend you don't see them coming after you .

To be brave…is to be hunted.

To be considered prey.

That fear been after me for a long time
That mind game, I've been playing a long time.

I keep winning. I keep waking up.

And To breathe. To put feet on the floor to be chased by the same mob that's been after you since 1997….that's courage.

It takes courage

To be silent in the middle of chaos in your mind.
To be silent in the middle of disturbance.
To be silent in the middle of you crumbling.

Because words will give it attention

To be brave is to operate with a constant duel perspective.
It's to have joy with sorrow whispering in endless chatter.

To be brave is to continue to walk though depression tries to
be your shadow. Tries to lurk in crevices of memories
To breathe when anxiety is screaming.
To rest when worry is daring you to a duel.

To be brave is to fight to live.

IX

Until Next Time

There will be a next time.

Before the Microphone

I have tried to "write happy" for years. Even in the most joyous occasions I would find it difficult to creatively write about what was obviously good. I've grown to love the gift of putting words to what could be perceived as heart wrenching and make it art. However; in this next poem of reflection I make note of how honorable it is to suffer and see the beauty come out of it. I remember the tough days where there were more tears than words and where loneliness was present in rooms full of people and praise. I love the imagery of there being a crossover in my writing from dark to palatable. The truth is, when performing most people see the art as beautiful, but look over the actual words and schemes. Others may scoff or try to redirect the topic to lighter subjects, but sometimes life isn't as flowery as we would like it and some stems have thorns. It's important to give space to the invitation of testimonies that come in poetic form. This piece is my celebration of being able to get through, and possibly cross over into happier writing.

Life on Display

Saginaw, E Lansing, Lansing, Ovid, Royal Oak…

My stories have littered cities.

Leaving evidence of my presence.
I didn't mean to pollute my surrounding areas instead,
what I once considered trash I intended to recycle.

Making treasure from the disposed
Art from ashes
canvases of color

I meant to Leave museums filled with my history.
And if my life were to be an exhibit, a display…
I mean If those instances were to be framed.
You would have to Handle the pieces delicately,
reading each description carefully.
My broken pieces salvaged to be the art of others eyes.
Call it a motion picture.

Because if I those happenings were to play in a movie…
you would see me tread the grounds of those spaces that hold

the depth of my circumstances.
You would see me eating of the fruit, even though the seed was painful.
You would see flowers sprouting through concrete

Speaking of flowers…
I've never been one for gardening
But my life caused growth to hearty willows.
I no longer feel the roots slithering into my heart.
I feel like the grass is greener because of my tears sprinkling the parched scorched soils of ruin.

I feel power
I feel that as I continue my steps are little more heavy and weighted
I feel like the champ, the victor of my past pains
I feel like I've arrived.
I've made it.

I've won heavenly awards for my performances
Stood on stages accepting the story.
With speeches that mimic:
Self: Thank you, I'm sorry I didn't believe in you sooner
Friends: Thank you, I'm sorry. I was grieving And I pray you have no context for it any time soon
Family: Thank you, I'm sorry. I pushed you away believing that if you were to leave it would hurt less
Opportunities: I'm sorry I listened to them
God: thank you for the pleasure of this role

So Let this poem be my bridge to happy writing.

We are over those troubled waters
The sky holds a rainbow of promise after floods
After storms
After hurricane

In conclusion,
My art, my life's feature presentation,
often lay on display before others.

And I'm proud of it.
I'm proud to turn melancholy to metaphor
Proud to bring creative depth to disaster
Proud to bring light to dark trenches
Proud of the dodged bullets
Proud of the arrows that lay at my feet.
I'm proud to survive what should've killed me.

I lived to write about it… and I will.

Acknowledgment

Husband: As always you're the best. Your never ending support allows me to keep pushing, and keep going to see where I can go. Thank you for being a great covering, listening ear, voice of reason, and partner in life!

Collective Verite: Before I met you ____, I was stuck in one genre, afraid of being "struck down" for writing anything else. I was afraid of not being accepted if I didn't rhyme. Afraid of not glorifying God if I wasn't "churchy" anymore. What you all helped me to realize is that to Glorify God in writing, you have to be real. TRUTH will give him glory and open up the conversation after the mic. Thank you for all of those writing challenges in 2017 that pushed me to be better and step outside of the box that I was in.

Aunt Tweekie: You've always been artistic, eccentric, creative and never hesitant to express yourself. Your freedom to be yourself gave your nieces and nephews safe spaces to dream outside of the norm. Thank you.

Jessica, Shannon, & Robert: You all delivered similar prophetic words to me about putting this project together. Two of which were on the same day MINUTES apart.Thank you for being obedient in speaking what the Lord revealed to you. The timing of your obedience is what pushed me to move forward.

About the Author

Brittney Davis was born and raised in Saginaw, MI. She is a spoken word artist, a member of the Collective Verite Poetry Collective, and the founder of Undefined...L.L.C. She prides herself on being undefinable. Brittney began writing through journaling as early as six years old as a means to cope with trauma, and later found a love for masking her pain and expressing herself through creative words. Her passions include using creativity to reach the unreachable and showing the love of Christ to those who need it the most. Through her writing she strives to let others know that they are not alone and she creates a safe space for those who deal with the pains of grief, heartache and life happenings. Brittney Charisse prides herself on being versatile and flexible with content in order to touch hearts and lead them to a greater resolve, Jesus. She has graced the stage in college classrooms, conferences, high schools, churches and local venues across the nation with one thing in mind: "What you say on stage is only half of your impact, but it's also about what you say when you step off of the stage."

You can connect with me on:
🌐 https://www.brittneycharisse.com

Also by Brittney Charisse

Fathered

Fathered is a metaphorical journey of spirituality. Brittney Davis Parallels the endearing relationship she shared with her now departed father with the relationship she is continually experiencing with God, the Father. She reveals to readers how having a close-knit, loving, supportive, corrective, and protective experience with her natural father helped her understand how God shows himself as Father to us in ways we sometimes don't recognize. God is not a detached ruler in the heavens who looks down in juedgement-he is present and his heart beats for his children.